THE KINGDOM

———

A STORY

VINNY COLAGIOVANNI

Xulon
PRESS

Copyright © 2010 by Vinny Colagiovanni

The Kingdom
A Story
by Vinny Colagiovanni

Printed in the United States of America

ISBN 9781612154558

www.xulonpress.com

To Heatheran,

    my daughter.

Remember the words

    of your mom,

        "Never lose your

        faith in God!"

Contents

Acknowledgments

I would like to thank Charlie, Mike, Dennis, Richard, Tom, Renee, Shirley, Alex and Clint who offered their time, encouragement and correction.

After a sleepless night, in the cool sunny morning, the crowd continued their search. They sought the one who had freely given. He had fed them yesterday and it was free. They had conversed among themselves jokingly, "Who said there is no such thing as a free lunch?" But now it was today and they were hungry again.

Suddenly, the search was over. For there he stood; a majestic looking man. "Royalty", spoke someone in the crowd. "Certainly this is a king", spoke another.

There was a mystery about the Giver that caused them to wonder, "Who is this man?"

They had heard him speak yesterday. Somehow, they wanted to believe the things he said. But would his principles and teachings work in the reality of real life? "Love your enemies and pray for them," the Giver proclaimed. How could such a teaching bring blessings or freedom, they thought. The Giver spoke of living exciting fearless lives; "Fear not, only believe." And could it be true, "If you do not forgive, you will not be forgiven!"

Nothing they had tried in the past had brought freedom. Could this be the opportunity they had searched for all their lives? These ideas needed to be pondered. But the true meaning of their search returned — they were hungry. However, they did not want the Giver to know the reason why they sought him. After all, he had fed them yesterday and it was free. And here they are today, looking for food again! The crowd, in their hunger, still had one thing — their pride.

So, looking pious they approached him, "Hello Giver, when did you get here?"

The Giver being filled with all knowledge replied, "You seek me not to see a miracle. You seek me not to get to know me. You seek me for food."

The group shuddered, "He knows what we are thinking."

The Giver spoke, "Do not look for physical food. Look for the spiritual food that gives everlasting life."

The crowd, sensing a feeling of freedom when he spoke, questioned him. "We seek this everlasting life, so how can we please God? What does God require of us? What work or task can we do for Him?"

The Giver replied, "You do not have to work to receive everlasting life. You must only believe in me, the one sent by God."

"Believe in you!!" said the crowd. "Believe in you??!! All we have to do is believe in you??!!"

"It's just that simple! Just believe in me!" replied the Giver.

"Believe I am who I say I am, the One sent by God. And believe I am able to do all things."

The crowd, perplexed by this strong statement said, "Our faith is low. What miracle or sign will you perform for us that we may see and believe that you are the One sent by God? It is recorded in the sacred writings, the prophet gave our ancestors food from heaven when they were hungry in the desert. Actual food appeared and our ancestors ate and were satisfied. You claim to be more than a prophet — the One sent by God. Certainly, it will be easy for you to perform a feat such as this."

The Giver spoke, "The prophet did not supply the food in the desert. God, the one who has sent me, gave the food from heaven in the desert. But far more exciting is the spiritual food that God sends from heaven. This spiritual food brings a life far greater than the life you are currently living. Today, you live a life of ordinary existence. The spiritual food brings days of overwhelming joy with a peace that cannot be explained in words."

The crowd of seekers raised their voices and replied, "Giver, give us this spiritual food! Help us, for we are a desperate needy people. We want to really live, not just exist. We seek something or someone who is truly real, not phony. All our lives we have searched for real freedom. We are sincere. We know there is more to life than we are experiencing. What we thought was freedom, turned out to be a counterfeit. This has left us unfulfilled. We heard you say that you are life. We ask for the life you speak about. Convince us that what you say is the truth."

"I am the way, the truth and the life," proclaimed the Giver. "I am life; real life. If you want to really live you must receive me. I am the spiritual food from heaven. Yesterday I gave you physical food hoping that you would receive my teaching and desire to know me. Today, you are looking for more physical food. You are unconcerned about having a relationship with me. Even now, as I speak of myself as the spiritual food from heaven, you, in your hearts, just want to eat. But I say unto you, I am the bread of life. If you believe on me and receive me you will never hunger or thirst. I speak the truth, for I am the truth. I cannot lie."

The Giver continued, "The supernatural is here. The new

age has arrived. The new kingdom is before you. Swallow your pride and increase your faith. Believe in me, the One sent from above, and receive the blessing of the new kingdom.

In times past, while searching for the truth, you overlooked me. Today, your search is over.

Do not push me aside. For again I say I am the spiritual food that satisfies. Only I can bring satisfaction. I, and I alone, can meet all your needs. All your lives, you have been searching for freedom. You said so yourselves. I am the One who can set you free. I am the bread of life! Real life! I am your freedom. Please do not walk away from freedom.

The church has not received the outcasts with the love of God. Some of you have experienced this rejection. Be assured, this is not my plan. Everyone is invited to my kingdom.

The church cannot set you free. In many cases, the local church has failed its people. Some churches have not taught people that they can know God, in a personal way.

I thank you for your good deeds. Always keep doing them. But more important than your good deeds -- get to know me!

Believe and receive me. Your journey has been desperate for too long. Let's end the pain. Come to me and I will give you rest. Please realize you are coming to me, not to a church. Again I say; it is not the church that sets you free. It is I and I alone.

You started out, as a child, with your dreams. Dreams of success, a good job and per-haps a family. Some of you, in the midst of all this, set out to find the so called secret of life. Some decided, "I am going to find God." You searched in sincerity, but to no avail. For God is a spirit and He must be sought spiritually. You may have attended church and went through all the rituals and ceremonies, knowing about God but never really knowing God. So you continued to live your lives without a real relationship with God. For some, life has been OK. But, as you have said, there is more to life than you are experiencing. Some of you have pined your years away. For others, your lives have been a disaster.

You may attend church regularly but there is no intimacy with God. You know there is a God. But you can only say, "I do not know Him."

Please, do not fear to know God in a personal way. He wants to bless you not hurt you. His kingdom is the highest, purest spiritual kingdom. But before you enter in, you must be purified. Its OK, everyone makes mistakes; there are no perfect people. Fear not, I will cleanse and purify you of all your wrong deeds. No matter what the wrong deeds are, I will cleanse you! There is nothing too hard for me to do!!

Do not try to cleanse yourself. It is impossible, only I can make you clean. God will not be fooled!! If you try to cleanse yourself, He will see

24

through your meager attempts to purify your lives. All that is required of you is faith in me to perform the task. This process must take place so I can present you as being faultless. Be advised, you are entering the true, holy super-natural. Today is the day to enter into the kingdom and receive the blessing! Do not think about where you are or your circumstances. Look to me and believe!"

The Giver continued, "Again I say to you, I fed you yesterday and here you are today looking for food. No matter what I offer you today in the spiritual realm; you just want to eat. So please allow me to say, I am the bread of life that has come down from heaven to do the will of the God. It is His desire that His created people enter into his kingdom."

The crowd murmured, among themselves, "How can this man say that he is the bread that came down from heaven? He was born of earthly parents, for we know his mother and father."

The Giver spoke, "Do not murmur among yourselves about where I came from. Remember this, he who believes in me has everlasting life. The bread from heaven that I speak of -

if you eat it you will never die! You will live forever!! I need your complete attention — the bread that I will give is my flesh."

The crowd became disturbed. They conversed among themselves saying, "How can this man give us his flesh to eat?"

The Giver proclaimed, "Unless you eat my flesh and drink my blood there is no real life in you. Whoever eats my flesh and drinks my blood, will not die! They will live forever! Whoever eats my flesh and drinks my blood, they live in me—and I live in them. This is not not the bread that your ancestors

ate in the desert. Your ancestors eventually died. If you
eat the bread I speak of, my
flesh, and drink my blood, you
will have everlasting life!"

The crowd, almost in anger
replied, "What you are saying
is hard for us to understand.
How can we eat your flesh and
drink your blood? This is an
unbelievable, foolish idea!"

The Giver declared, "Does
eating my flesh and drinking
my blood offend you? Please,
allow me to explain. It is the
spirit that gives everlasting
life, the flesh is of no value."

The crowd puzzled by his
answer questioned the Giver,

"The flesh is of no value!!??
The flesh is of no value!!??
You have been telling us, that
unless we eat your flesh and
drink your blood there is no
real life in us. Now you say
the flesh is of no value. This
contradiction confuses us!"

The Giver spoke, "There is
no contradiction!

This morning you sought
me looking for food. Food is
important, but there is so much
more that I want to give you.
I tried to steer the conversation away from physical food.
I wanted to give you the spiritual food that gives everlasting life. But you, thinking

everything has a cost, wanted to know what work you could perform to attain the spiritual food. But you cannot work for or buy the spiritual food. As I told you, 'just believe in me' to receive the spiritual food. Then you brought the conversation back to physical food, pointing to your ancestors who ate the miracle food in the desert. You remained fixed on the goal of your journey, to find physical food. For me to gain your attention, for you to listen to anything I have said, I have had to speak of myself as that which you are looking for — food and drink.

For this reason, I spoke of my flesh as food and my blood as drink. However, I was speaking to you in spiritual terms. I do not want you to physically eat my flesh and drink my blood. I want you to receive me spiri- tually — with your hearts.

A disturbance arose in the crowd. "You have lied to us!" shouted one. "Deceiver!" yelled another. "You have played us!" continued the crowd. Taunts and threats began to arise. The crowd became emotionally hurt and prideful.

The Giver spoke, "I have not played you. I have communicated with you at the level of your

understanding; your understanding being food. Please,
do not be offended.

I had to show you your inner
selves. I do not want you to
continue to live your lives
with shallow motives and pride.
My desire, in exposing your
inner hearts, is that you be
set free. I want you to live
fulfilled lives of freedom. At
the end of this earthly life, I
do not want any of you saying,
'I never really lived.' Believe
and receive me. I cannot lie for
I am the truth. Do not fear the
freedom. The offer remains."

Many of the crowd became
bitter for the Giver had exposed

their wrong motives and pride. Suddenly, one member of the crowd turned and walked away — followed by another. A steady stream of the Givers' followers left him — never to return. With their feelings hurt, they would not give-up their wrong motives and pride.

THE INVITATION

We are standing at the threshold of His kingdom. The question arises, what will we do with the Givers' offer of freedom? Will we give up our pride and self-sufficiency and admit that we need help? If we do, we will truly begin to live. The Giver is Jesus Christ. If you do not know Him as your Lord, I ask that you would believe on Him today. Believe that He is the Son of the living God. Believe that He is the only one who can purify you. He will bless you, open your eyes and set you free.

Please pray this or a similar prayer: Jesus, I believe that you are the Son of the living God. I have made mistakes in my life. I have lived my life, my way. For this reason, I ask for forgiveness. I need you to purify me and make me ready for your kingdom — here on earth, as well as in heaven. Jesus, by the act of my will, I come close to You. I spiritually receive you into my heart.

So be it, amen.

*** Epilogue ***

ᕫᕫ

To my Roman Catholic brothers and sisters,

I took the preceding story from the Holy Bible, the book of John, chapter 6, verses 25-66. In the story, Jesus listened to the crowds' request for food and looked at their behavior. He then decided what type of psychology or mental strategy to use to communicate with the crowd.

The crowds' main reason for their search was to find food. So, as a figure of speech, Jesus spoke of himself as food, ('I am the bread of life...'), ('unless you eat my flesh...), to attract the crowd's attention. Jesus drew the crowd into His teaching by referring to His flesh and blood as food and drink. When He had their attention, He reversed His teaching, in the preceding story, stating,

"It is spirit that gives everlasting life, the flesh is of no value."

Some of the members of the crowd did not like Jesus' teaching tactics. They felt betrayed. For this reason, many of the crowd left Him and no longer walked with Him.

In a similar story, at the last supper, Jesus took the bread and said, "This is my body…" Jesus also took the cup and said, "This is my blood…"

None of the apostles asked for an explanation of the words of Jesus. The apostles were present earlier when Jesus spoke figuratively to the crowd that was seeking physical food. At that time Jesus stated, "The flesh profits nothing." Jesus wanted

them to receive Him spiritually, with their hearts.

The apostles, before Jesus
went to the cross, did not know
what the communion service
represented. But after Jesus
died and was resurrected, the
apostles remembered the words
of Jesus to re-enact the last
supper, 'This is my body… do
this in remembrance of Me.' The
apostles understood, after the
resurrection, that the communion service was a remembrance
or memorial to His death on the
cross. During the communion
service Jesus would be present
spiritually but not physically.

However, the Roman Catholic church teaches that during the mass, the gifts of bread and wine are changed in to the actual body (flesh) and blood of Jesus. The changed gifts are distributed and eaten by the parishioners. In the Bible, the actual words of Jesus are not in agreement with the Roman Catholic church's teaching on communion. Now the question arises, do we want to believe the words of Jesus Christ or the teaching of the Roman Catholic church. God wants us to know the truth!

Please do not misunderstand me. This is not an attack on

the Roman Catholic church. I know it is a great and majestic church. This cannot be denied. It has existed for nearly 2,000 years. However, the Roman Catholic church is made of human beings and human beings make mistakes. False ideas and false concepts can find their way into any group or organization.

Jesus warned of false teachings in the church; rules and laws that are actually man-made commandments. Saints Peter and Paul were the "watch-dogs" of the early churches' rules and laws. Whenever a church moved away from the simplicity of Jesus, they corrected the church in a loving manner. We can see this in the new testament epistles (letters). However, after Saints Peter and Paul passed on, the new leaders must not have held on to the simple gospel, and allowed false teaching to enter into the church. The modern church leaders cannot be blamed for this inherited problem. It has been handed down from generation to generation.

However, the false teaching on communion, needs to be addressed and changed. False teaching should not be allowed in our lives, for it weighs us down like heavy baggage and robs us of God's greatest blessings.

My Roman Catholic brothers and sisters, let's pray and believe that, in our lifetime, the Roman Catholic church will return to the simplicity of it's early church beginnings. I believe God would be greatly pleased!

Some of you may be saying, "I don't care what communion is, it doesn't matter to me. If it was good enough for my parents and grandparents, its good enough for me. I just believe what the priests say." I can understand what you're saying. It's a busy life. But you owe it to yourself and your family to hear and study the truth and then act accordingly.

You might be saying, "What should I do?" I would suggest you read, the two Bible versions included at the end of this book. These Scriptures tell the story of Jesus and the crowd. This will help to get a 'feel' and understanding of the psychology Jesus used on the crowd.

The two versions, are in Appendix A and B of this book. The first version is a modern version. The second version, of the story of Jesus and the crowd, is from the Douay-

Rheims Bible, upon which some versions of the Roman Catholic Bible are based. Pray, before you read Appendix A and B, that the Holy Spirit will give you wisdom and show you the truth concerning Holy Communion.

I would also suggest that you pray and ask God what you should do. Then when you know, in your heart that God is leading you, obey His instructions. But first, make sure you know it is God's will for your life.

Obedience, to Gods' plans for our lives, brings great blessings! I do not want anyone to feel they are being thrown into a "spiritual crisis." Just pray and obey!

Lets leave a heritage of the truth to our children, grand-children and all the following generations.

Now that we know the truth in the matter of communion, let's receive communion in deep spiritual gratitude.

Any further investigation or debate on the subject of communion is unnecessary. Just look at the simple words of Jesus in the book of John, chapter 6, verse 63, (verse 64 in older catholic bibles):

"It is the spirit that
gives life; the flesh
profits nothing: the words
I speak to you are spirit
and they are life."

And may I add, Jesus' words
are "real life."

There is a challenge to all
who read this book. With your
new understanding of communion, will you ask the church
leaders to bring the churches'
teaching on communion into har-
mony with the words of Jesus?

Church leaders will you act on
this information or just sweep
it under the rug and allow the
church to remain in a lukewarm

state? May I humbly say, God will hold you accountable! I am praying you make the right decision.

And now Jesus, I pray for all who read this book. Please bring them to your truth.

Life is short, let's live it in freedom. To live our lives dwelling in His kingdom, is a privilege. Let's live in the kingdom without false teachings.

Remember, my Catholic brothers and sisters, the truth will set us free. By the truth, the church will be set free!!!

APPENDICES

APPENDIX A

❧❧

This appendix is the NEW CENTURY VERSION bible, book of John, Chapter 6, verses 25-66.

25 When the people found Jesus on the other side of the lake, they asked him, "Teacher, when did you come here?"

26 Jesus answered, "I tell you the truth, you aren't looking for me because you saw me do

miracles. You are looking for me because you ate the bread and were satisfied.

27 Don't work for the food that spoils. Work for the food that stays good always and gives eternal life. The Son of Man will give you this food, because on him God the Father has put his power."

28 The people asked Jesus, "What are the things God wants us to do?"

29 Jesus answered, "The work God wants you to do is this: Believe the One he sent."

30 So the people asked, "What miracle will you do? If we see a miracle, we will believe you. What will you do?

31 Our ancestors ate the manna in the desert. This is written in the Scriptures: 'He gave them bread from heaven to eat.'

32 Jesus said, "I tell you the truth, it was not Moses who gave you bread from heaven; it is my Father who is giving you the true bread from heaven.

33 God's bread is the One who comes down from heaven and gives life to the world."

34 The people said, "Sir, give us this bread always."

35 Then Jesus said, "I am the bread that gives life. Whoever comes to me will never be hungry, and whoever believes in me will never be thirsty.

36 But as I told you before, you have seen me and still don't believe.

37 The Father gives me the people who are mine. Every one of them will come to me, and I will always accept them.

38 I came down from heaven to do what God wants me to do, not what I want to do.

39 Here is what the One who sent me wants me to do: I must not lose even one whom God gave me, but I must raise them all on the last day.

40 Those who see the Son and believe in him have eternal life, and I will raise them on the last day. This is what my Father wants."

41 Some people began to complain about Jesus because he

said, "I am the bread that comes down from heaven."

42 They said, "This is Jesus, the son of Joseph. We know his father and mother. How can he Say, 'I came down from heaven?'"

43 But Jesus answered, "Stop complaining to each other.

44 The Father is the One who sent me. No one Can come to me unless the Father draws him to me, and I will raise that person up on the last day.

45 It is written in the prophets, 'They will all be taught by

God.' Everyone who listens to the Father and learns from him comes to me.

46 No one has seen the Father except the One who is from God; only He has seen the Father.

47 I tell you the truth, who-ever believes has eternal life.

48 I am the bread that gives life.

49 Your ancestors ate the manna in the desert, but still they died.

50 Here is the bread that comes down from heaven. Anyone who eats this bread will never die.

51 I am the living bread that came down from heaven. Anyone who eats this bread will live forever. This bread is my flesh, which I will give up so that the world may have life."

52 Then the evil people began to argue among themselves, saying, "How can this man give us his flesh to eat?"

53 Jesus said, "I tell you the truth, you must eat the flesh of the Son of Man and drink his

blood. Otherwise, you won't have real life in you.

54 Those who eat my flesh and drink my blood have eternal life, and I will raise them up on the last day.

55 My flesh is true food, and my blood is true drink.

56 Those who eat my flesh and drink my blood live in me, and I live in them.

57 The living Father sent me, and I live because of the Father. So whoever eats me will live because of me.

58 I am not like the bread your ancestors ate. They ate that bread and still died. I am the bread that came down from heaven, and whoever eats this bread will live forever."

59 Jesus said all these things while he was teaching in the synagogue in Capernaum.

THE WORDS OF ETERNAL LIFE

60 When the followers of Jesus heard this, many of them said, "This teaching is hard. Who can accept it?"

61 Knowing that his followers were complaining about this, Jesus said, "Does this teaching bother you?

62 Then will it also bother you to see the Son of Man going back to the place where he came from?

63 It is the Spirit that gives life. The flesh doesn't give life. The words I told you are spirit, and they give life.

64 But some of you don't believe." (Jesus knew from the beginning who did not believe

and who would turn against him.)

65 Jesus said, "That is the reason I said, 'If the Father does not bring a person to me, that one cannot come.'"

66 After Jesus said this, many of his followers left him and stopped following him.

APPENDIX B

⚜

This appendix is the DOUAY-RHEIMS bible, book of John, chapter 6, verses 25-66.

25 And when they had found him on the other side of the sea, they said to him: Rabbi, when camest thou hither?

26 Jesus answered them, and said: Amen, amen I say to you, you seek me, not because you

have seen miracles, but because you did eat of the loaves, and were filled.

27 Labour not for the meat which perisheth, but for that which endureth unto life ever-lasting, which the Son of Man will give you. For him hath God, the Father, sealed.

28 They said therefore unto him: What shall we do, that we may work the works of God?

29 Jesus answered, and said to them: This is the work of God, that you believe in him whom he hath sent.

30 They said therefore to him: What sign therefore dost thou shew, that we may see, and may believe thee? What dost thou work?

31 Our Fathers did eat manna in the desert, as it is written: He gave them bread from heaven to eat.

32 Then Jesus said to them: Amen, amen I say to you; Moses gave you not bread from heaven, but my Father giveth you the true bread from heaven.

33 For the bread of God is that which cometh down from heaven, and giveth life to the world.

34 They said therefore unto him: Lord, give us always this bread.

35 And Jesus said to them: I am the bread of life: he that cometh to me shall not hunger: and he that believeth in me shall never thirst.

36 But I say unto you, that you also have seen me, and you believe not.

37 All that the Father giveth to me shall come to me; and him that cometh to me, I will not cast out.

38 Because I came down from heaven, not to do my own will, but the will of him that sent me.

39 Now this is the will of the Father who sent me: that of all that he hath given me, I should lose nothing; but should raise it up again in the last day.

40 And this is the will of my Father that sent me: that every one who seeth the Son,

and believeth in him, may have life everlasting, and I will raise him up in the last day.

41 The Jews therefore murmured at him, because he had said: I am the living bread which came down from heaven.

42 And they said: Is not this Jesus, the son of Joseph, whose father and mother we know? How then saith he, I came down from heaven?

43 Jesus therefore answered, and said to them: Murmur not among yourselves.

44 No man can come to me, except the Father, who hath sent me, draw him; and I will raise him up in the last day.

45 It is written in the prophets: And they shall all be taught of God. Every one that hath heard of the Father, and hath learned, cometh to me.

46 Not that any man hath seen the Father; but he who is of God, he hath seen the Father.

47 Amen, amen I say unto you: He that believeth in me, hath everlasting life.

48 I am the bread of life.

49 Your Fathers did eat manna in the desert, and are dead.

50 This is the bread which cometh down from heaven; that if any man eat of it, he may not die.

51 I am the living bread which came down from heaven.

52 If any man eat of this bread, he shall live for ever; and the bread that I will give, is my flesh, for the life of the world.

53 The Jews therefore strove among themselves, saying: How can this man give us his flesh to eat?

54 Then Jesus said to them: Amen, amen I say unto you: Except you eat the flesh of the Son of man, and drink his blood, you shall not have life in you.

55 He that eateth my flesh, and drinketh my blood, hath everlasting life: and I will raise him up in the last day.

56 For my flesh is meat indeed: and my blood is drink indeed.

57 He that eateth my flesh, and drinketh my blood, abideth in me, and I in him.

58 As the living Father hath sent me, and I live by the Father; so he that eateth me, the same also shall live by me.

59 This is the bread that came down from heaven. Not as your Fathers did eat manna, and are dead. He that eateth this bread, shall live for ever.

60 These things he said, teaching in the synagogue, in Capharnaum.

61 Many therefore of his disciples, hearing it, said: This saying is hard, and who can hear it?

62 But Jesus, knowing in himself, that his disciples murmured at this, said to them: Doth this scandalize you?

63 If then you shall see the Son of man ascend up where he was before?

64 It is the spirit that quickeneth: the flesh profiteth nothing. The words that I have spoken to you, are spirit and life.

65 But there are some of you that believe not. For Jesus knew from the beginning, who they were that did not believe, and who he was, that should betray him.

66 And he said: Therefore did I say to you, that no man can come to me, unless it be given him by my Father.

67 After this many of his disciples went back and walked no more with him.

NOTES

NOTES

NOTES

NOTES

CPSIA information can be obtained at www.ICGtesting.com
Printed in the USA
BVOW021950280312

286313BV00001B/33/P

9 781612 154558